Dinosaurs

Diplodocus

Daniel Nunn

Heinemann Library
Chicago, Illinois

Customer Service 888-454-2279
Visit our website at www.heinemannraintree.com

Designed by Joanna Hinton-Malivoire
Printed and bound in China by South China Printing Co. Ltd.

11 10 09 08 07
10 9 8 7 6 5 4 3 2 1

The Library of Congress has cataloged the first edition of this book as follows:
Nunn, Daniel.
  Diplodocus / Daniel Nunn.
     p. cm. -- (Dinosaurs)
  Includes bibliographical references and index.
  ISBN-13: 978-1-4034-9447-4 (library binding - hardcover)
  ISBN-13: 978-1-4034-9454-2 (pbk.)
  1. Diplodocus--Juvenile literature. I. Title.
  QE862.S3N864 2007
  567.913--dc22
                                    2006030057

Acknowledgements
The publishers would like to thank the following for permission to reproduce photographs: Alamy pp. 21 and 22 (blickwinkel); Corbis pp. 6 (Zefa/ Peter Adams), 7 and 23 (Zefa/Harald Lange), 18 (Ted Soqui), 22 (Craig Lovell); Getty Images pp. 20 and 23 (The Image Bank/Grant Faint); Science Photo Library p. 19 (Joyce Photographics).

Cover photograph of Diplodocus reproduced with permission of Corbis/Harald Lange/zefa.

Every effort has been made to contact copyright holders of any material reproduced in this book. Any omissions will be rectified in subsequent printings if notice is given to the publishers.

Contents

The Dinosaurs

Dinosaurs were reptiles.

Dinosaurs lived long ago.

Diplodocus was a dinosaur.
Diplodocus lived long ago.

Today there are no *Diplodocus*.

Diplodocus

Some dinosaurs were small.

But *Diplodocus* was very big.

Diplodocus had a long tail.

Diplodocus had strong legs.

Diplodocus had a very long neck.

Diplodocus had a small head.

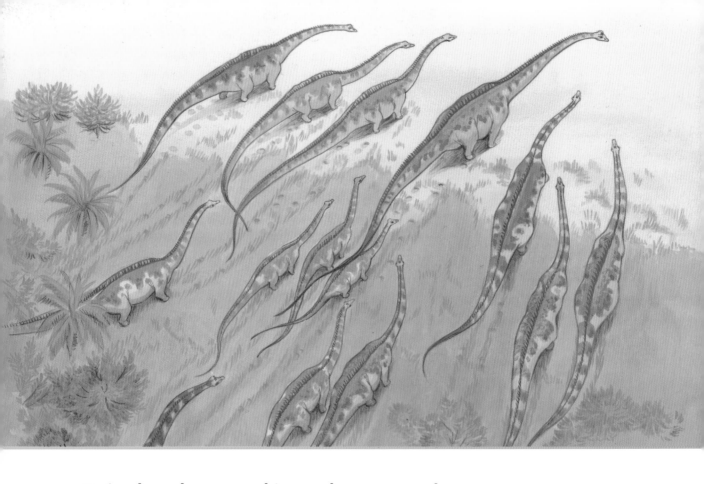

Diplodocus lived together.

Diplodocus ate plants.

Other dinosaurs attacked *Diplodocus*.

Diplodocus used its tail to
fight back.

How Do We Know?

Scientists have found fossils
of *Diplodocus*.

Fossils are parts of animals that lived long ago.

fossil

Fossils are in rocks.

Fossils tell us what *Diplodocus* was like.

Fossil Quiz

One of these fossils was *Diplodocus*.
Can you tell which one?

Picture Glossary

dinosaur an animal that lived long ago

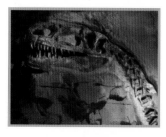
fossil parts of a dead animal that lived long ago

reptile animal that is cold-blooded. Snakes, lizards, turtles, and alligators are reptiles.

Answer to question on page 22
Fossil A was *Diplodocus*.
Fossil B was *Tyrannosaurus rex*.

Index

Notes to Parents and Teachers

This series gives a first introduction to dinosaurs. In simple language, each book explains the physical characteristics of different dinosaurs, their behavior, and how fossils have provided a key into our knowledge of dinosaurs' existence and extinction. An expert was consulted to provide both interesting and accurate content. The text has been carefully chosen with the advice of a literacy expert to ensure that beginners can read the text independently or with moderate support.

You can support children's nonfiction literacy skills by helping students use the table of contents, picture glossary, and index.